Why Catholic?
Journey through the Catechism

Christian Prayer: Deepening My Experience of God

The publisher gratefully acknowledges use of the following:

The Scripture quotations contained herein are from the New Revised Standard Version Bible, copyright © 1989 by the Division of Christian Education of the National Council of the Churches of Christ in the U.S.A., and are used by permission. All rights reserved.

English translation of the *Catechism of the Catholic Church*, for the United States of America Copyright © 1994, United States Catholic Conference, Inc. - Libreria Editrice Vaticana. English translation of the *Catechism of the Catholic Church: Modifications from the Editio Typica* Copyright © 1997, United States Catholic Conference, Inc. - Libreria Editrice Vaticana. Used with permission.

Copyright permission for posting of the translation of the *Catechism of the Catholic Church* on the RENEW International Web site was granted by "Administrazione del Patrimonio della Sede Apostolica," case number 344.333 on May 14, 2001, Vatican City. For online access to the full text of the *Catechism of the Catholic Church*, go to www.ParishLife.com/*Catechism*.htm. This is an interactive site allowing users to search the official *Catechism* text.

The prayer on page 5 is reprinted or adapted with permission from *Prayers for a Planetary Pilgrim* by Father Edward Hays, copyright Forest of Peace Publishing, 251 Muncie Road, Leavenworth, KS 66048.

Nihil Obstat
Reverend Lawrence E. Frizzell, D.Phil.
Archdiocese of Newark Theological Commission
Censor Librorum

IMPRIMATUR
Most Reverend John J. Myers, D.D., J.C.D.
Archbishop of Newark

Cover design by James F. Brisson

Library of Congress Control Number: 2002091633

ISBN 1-930978-17-0

Published by RENEW International Publications
1232 George Street
Plainfield, New Jersey 07062-1717
Phone   908-769-5400
www.renewintl.org
www.ParishLife.com

Printed and bound in the United States of America.

Contents

† † †

Introduction iii

Session 1 .... What Is Prayer? 1

Session 2 .... Prayer in the Old Testament 7

Session 3   Jesus and Mary Teach Us to Pray 13

Session 4   Forms of Prayer 17

Session 5   The Sources and Way of Prayer 22

Session 6   Guides for Prayer 27

Session 7   Vocal Prayer and Meditation 31

Session 8   Contemplative Prayer 36

Session 9   Difficulties in Prayer 39

Session 10   The Lord's Prayer 44

Session 11   The Lord's Prayer (continued) 48

Session 12   The Lord's Prayer (continued) 53

Music Resources 59

Acknowledgments

✝ ✝ ✝

RENEW International acknowledges all who helped make this small group resource possible, in particular, members of the small faith communities who piloted the materials and offered very helpful input.

Foreword
† † †

My calling as a bishop challenges me to ever seek means to assist solid faith formation and growth in holiness. Foundational in meeting this need is the *Catechism of the Catholic Church,* which so magnificently conveys the wisdom of the Holy Spirit in guiding the Church's tradition in following Jesus Christ.

The Introduction to the U.S. bishops' document "Our Hearts Were Burning Within Us" speaks of how disciples of Jesus share in proclaiming the Good News to all the world.

> Every disciple of the Lord Jesus shares in this mission. To do their part, adult Catholics must be mature in faith and well equipped to share the Gospel, promoting it in every family circle, in every church gathering, in every place of work, and in every public forum. They must be women and men of prayer whose faith is alive and vital, grounded in a deep commitment to the person and message of Jesus.

Why Catholic? A Journey through the Catechism is well designed to enable this goal to become reality. It faithfully breaks open the contents of the *Catechism* for reflection and assimilation by individuals or participants in small faith-sharing groups. The sharing enables participants to take greater personal ownership of their faith and to move from an inherited faith to deep faith conviction.

This exploration of divinely revealed truth has a formative effect on peoples' lives. The "yes" of consent to faith emulates Mary's fiat, her "yes" to God's will. A prayerful openness to God's will is the path to holiness.

Why Catholic? seeks to be an instrument for faith formation and a call to holiness. Saints in everyday life are the strength of the Church, which is always renewing itself in fidelity to the mission of Christ and in service to the needs of our society. I heartily commend this effort in making the *Catechism of the Catholic Church* more accessible to the faithful.

Most Reverend John J. Myers, J.C.D., D.D.
Archbishop of Newark

Introduction

Many Catholics have inherited the faith without knowing why they are Catholic. They have never been exposed to the solid faith formation provided by the *Catechism of the Catholic Church*. For that reason, RENEW International has taken the four parts of the *Catechism* and has developed this series, *Why Catholic? Journey through the Catechism*.

Why Catholic? is an easy-to-use tool for individuals and/or small faith-sharing communities to reference, read, pray over, and treasure the rich resources of the *Catechism of the Catholic Church*. By using these materials, we hope participants will study the *Catechism of the Catholic Church* in greater depth, internalize its teachings, share faith in Jesus Christ, learn more about their faith, and let their faith illuminate every aspect of their lives.

The reflections offer people a "taste" of the content of the *Catechism. Why Catholic?* is not intended to be a compendium or a total summary of the *Catechism*, but rather, a way for people to try to become more faithful to the teachings of the Church. We encourage people to read sections of the *Catechism* before, during, and after each session.

In a way, *Why Catholic?* is a guidebook to the *Catechism*. Yet it is much more. It invites readers and participants to a mature faith by nourishing and strengthening laywomen and men in their calling and identity as people of faith.

These four booklets may be a way for people to uncover their own story, their own journey about being Catholic. What does it mean to be Catholic? Why they stay? Why they became Catholic? To assist in discovering their story, we recommend participants keep a journal and after each session spend some time journaling key beliefs of the Catholic Church and their personal insights. What a valuable treasure they will have to meditate on and perhaps share with others.

Part One of the *Catechism of the Catholic Church* focuses on the great mysteries of our faith. In Part Two the emphasis is on celebrating our faith in sacramental liturgy. Part Three helps to explain the moral teachings of the Catholic faith. Part Four looks more deeply at our relationship with God and how we nurture that relationship in prayer.

The first few sessions of this book, *Christian Prayer,* focus on prayer itself and how God communicates with us. The next sessions look at different forms of prayer and some difficulties we experience in prayer. The last sessions offer a deeper look at the prayer that Jesus taught us, the Lord's Prayer. We will not just look at what the *Catechism* says about prayer; rather, we will use various styles of prayer in the sessions.

If you are gathering in a small community, you may wish to meet either in two six-week blocks of time or over twelve consecutive weeks to cover all the sessions. Your community may also wish to use the other three booklets based on the other parts of the *Catechism—The Profession of Faith* (Part One), *The Celebration of the Christian Mystery* (Part Two), and *Life in Christ* (Part Three).

May these reflections lead you to a closer, more vibrant relationship with our loving God.

Faith-Sharing Principles and Guidelines

When we gather as Christians to share our faith and grow together in community, it is important that we adhere to certain principles. The following Theological Principles and Small Community Guidelines will keep your community focused and help you to grow in faith, hope, and love.

Principles

- Each person is led by God on his or her spiritual journey. This happens in the context of the Christian community.
- Christ, the Word made flesh, is the root of Christian faith. It is because of, in, and through Christ that we come together to share our faith.
- Faith sharing refers to the shared reflections on the action of God in one's life experience as related to Scripture and the faith of the Church. Faith sharing is not discussion, problem solving, or Scripture study. The purpose is an encounter between a person in the concrete circumstances of one's life and a loving God, leading to a conversion of heart.
- The entire faith-sharing process is an expression of prayerful reflection.

Guidelines

- Constant attention to respect, honesty, and openness for each person will assist the community's growth.
- Each person shares on the level where he or she feels comfortable.
- Silence is a vital part of the total process. Participants are given time to reflect before any sharing begins, and a period of comfortable silence might occur between individual sharings.
- Persons are encouraged to wait to share a second time until others have contributed who wish to do so.
- The entire community is responsible for participating and faith sharing.
- Confidentiality is essential, allowing each person to share honestly.
- Action flowing out of the small community meetings is essential for the growth of individuals and the community.

A Note to Small Community Leaders

Small Community Leaders are...

- People who encourage participation and the sharing of our Christian faith.
- People who encourage the spiritual growth of the community and of the individual members through communal prayer and a prayerful atmosphere at meetings and through daily commitments by community members to prayer and reflection on the Scriptures.
- People who move the community to action to be carried out between meetings. They are not satisfied with a self-centered comfort level in the community but are always urging that the faith of the community be brought to impact on their daily lives and the world around them.
- Community builders who create a climate of hospitality and trust among all participants.

Small Community Leaders are not...

- **Theologians:** The nature of the meeting is faith sharing, therefore, should a theological or scriptural question arise, the leader should turn to the pastor or pastoral staff person to seek guidance.
- **Counselors:** The small communities are not intended to be problem solving. This is an inappropriate setting to deal with emotionally laden issues of a personal nature. The leader is clearly not to enter the realm of treating people with their emotional, in-depth feelings such as depression, anxiety, and intense anger. When someone moves in this direction, beyond faith sharing, the leader should bring the community back to faith sharing. With the help of the pastor and/or the pastoral staff, the person should be advised to seek the assistance of professional counseling.
- **Teachers:** The leaders are not teachers. Their role is to guide the process of the faith sharing as outlined in the materials.

How to Use This Booklet

Whenever two or more of us gather in the name of Jesus, we are promised that Christ is in our midst (See Matthew 18:20). This booklet helps communities to reflect on the Scriptures and the *Catechism of the Catholic Church*. It is most helpful if some members of the group or the group as a whole have the Scriptures and the *Catechism* at their meeting.

Those who have met in small communities will be familiar with the process. In this booklet based on the *Catechism*, however, there is particular emphasis on our relationship with God in prayer. These reflections make demands upon our reflective nature and help in the formation of our Catholic values. THEREFORE, IT IS IMPORTANT THAT PARTICIPANTS CAREFULLY PREPARE FOR THE SESSION BEFORE COMING TO THE MEETING. They are encouraged to read and reflect on the session itself, the Scripture passage(s) cited, and the sections of the *Catechism* referenced.

If the community has not met before or if participants do not know each other, take time for introductions and to get acquainted. People share most easily when they feel comfortable and accepted in a community.

Prayer must always be at the heart of our Christian gatherings. Most sessions begin with an Lifting Our Hearts. There are suggested songs, some of which may be found in the parish worship aid. Other songs may be used, such as *RENEW the Face of the Earth,* a three-part set available from Oregon Catholic Press Publications (OCP), 5536 NE Hassalo, Portland, OR 97213, Telephone: 800-LITURGY (800-548-8749).

Each week an action—Living the Good News—is recommended. This allows the participant to bring the reflection into his or her daily life and act upon it during the week. After the first week, the leader may wish to ask participants to share how they did with their Living the Good News from the previous session.

Following the Introductions, a prayer—Lifting Our Hearts—and the sharing of previous actions—Living the Good News—there is an initial Reflection on the *Catechism* followed by a Scripture passage that will give the community members the opportunity to reflect on what Jesus has said and to share their faith on the particular topic. Sharing could take about 15 minutes.

After reflecting on the Scriptures, there is time for additional Exploring the *Catechism* itself. Some sentences are direct quotes from the

Catechism. The direct quotes are in bold print. Some of the material is summarized and paraphrased; whether directly quoted or paraphrased, material from the *Catechism* is identified by the paragraph number from the *Catechism* in parentheses, that is, **(000).**

Following these Reflections there are Sharing Our Faith questions—allow approximately 30 minutes for the sharing. Faith sharing groups vary greatly in their background and composition. In some sessions, the group may wish to start with the following question: What insights into my faith did I gain from this session? Explain.

Each session offers some ideas for an action—Living the Good News; however, these are merely suggestions. It is important that group members choose an action that is both measurable and realistic.

Each session concludes with prayer—Lifting Our Hearts.

Suggested Format of the Sharing Sessions (1½ hours)

Introductions	(when the group is new or when someone joins the group)
10 min.	Lifting Our Hearts
5 min.	Living the Good News from previous sharing session
10 min.	Exploring the *Catechism*
15 min.	Scripture Passage and Sharing Question
10 min.	Continued Exploring the *Catechism*
25 min.	Sharing Our Faith
5 min.	Living the Good News
10 min.	Lifting Our Hearts

Session 1
What Is Prayer?

† † †

Suggested environment
Bible, candle, and, if possible, the *Catechism of the Catholic Church*
Begin with a quiet, reflective atmosphere.

Lifting Our Hearts

Song
"You Are Near," Dan Schutte, Oregon Catholic Press Publications (OCP)

Pray together

Father of love,
we come now to rest in you.
Our days and weeks are filled
with rushing and busyness.
But now, O Father,
we want, we need
to take this time to recollect ourselves,
to reestablish our priorities,
and to spend time with you,
our Creator and friend.

Help us to be calm,
to sit in your presence,
to ponder how much you love us
and are waiting for us to come to you.

Increase our faith and hope
in your Son Jesus Christ.
We know he is present with us.
We thank you for his presence
and his everlasting love.
Holy Spirit of love,
give us a great desire to pray,
to develop that intimacy that you desire with us.

1

Keep us always in your love and grace.
We ask this in the name of Jesus Christ
and in the power of the Holy Spirit. Amen

Exploring the *Catechism*

In the New Covenant, prayer is the living relationship of the children of God with their Father who is good beyond measure, with his Son Jesus Christ and with the Holy Spirit. The grace of the Kingdom is "the union of the entire holy and royal Trinity…with the whole human spirit" (2565). Prayer is God's loving gift to us of himself.

When we love someone, we give our heart to that person. We see the face of our beloved in so many ways. We want to be with our beloved and to share our life. The same could be said about prayer. Prayer is the language of a loving covenant—of a love for God who made us and continues to call us into a personal loving relationship. St. Thérèse of Lisieux has given us a beautiful description of prayer: "For me, prayer is a surge of the heart; it is a simple look turned toward heaven, it is a cry of recognition and of love, embracing both trial and joy" **(2558).** Thérèse's love for God was so full that she gave her heart totally.

In prayer, God gives himself to us and we give ourselves to God. We speak, listen, and respond to him. Prayer is the meeting of two loves—God and ourselves. God asks for our hearts completely. When we pray, we are asked to pray with humble hearts, not with hearts full of pride. **Only when we humbly acknowledge that "we do not know how to pray as we ought" (Romans 8:26) are we ready to receive freely the gift of prayer.** When we are humble, we see ourselves as we truly are. We are not God, but we depend upon God for our life and our love. St. Augustine reminds us that we all are beggars before him **(2559).**

Listen to the story of the Pharisee and the tax collector in Luke's Gospel as Jesus tells us to give our hearts fully to God in all humility.

Scripture: Pondering the Word   Luke 18:9–14

Sharing Question

- What stance do I take in prayer? Am I humble, fearful, confident, etc.?

2

Continued Exploring the *Catechism*

[T]he life of prayer is the habit of being in the presence of the thrice-holy God and in communion with him (2565). Prayer is a relationship. It is not something we do as much as being with someone we love. Oftentimes today we are busy with many things. We have jobs to do, children to raise, cleaning or gardening to do, gyms to go to, friends to see, television to watch, shopping to do. As a culture, we tend to place a great emphasis on our activities and accomplishments. We sometimes have trouble relaxing and just taking it easy. We know, however, that no love relationship grows unless we spend time with the person we love. That's what we do in prayer. We spend time with God, speaking and listening, offering our hearts to the one we love.

We are reminded in the gospel story of the Samaritan woman about the power of God: "If you knew the gift of God!" (John 4:10). **The wonder of prayer is revealed beside the well where we come seeking water: there, Christ comes to meet every human being. It is he who first seeks us and asks us for a drink.... Whether we realize it or not, prayer is the encounter of God's thirst with ours (2560).** Prayer is a foundational response of faith and a response of love to a God who longs for us **(2561).**

Where does prayer come from? Scripture speaks at times about prayer coming from the spirit or the soul, but most often, Scripture tells us, prayer comes from the heart. **If our heart is far from God, the words of prayer are in vain (2562). The heart is the dwelling-place where I am, where I live....** Our hearts are our inner selves, **our hidden center...; only the Spirit of God can fathom the human heart and know it fully. The heart is the place of decision.... It is the place of truth, where we choose life or death. It is the place of encounter, because as image of God we live in relation: it is the place of covenant (2563).**

Christian prayer is a covenant relationship between the Holy Trinity and ourselves **(2564).** As we lift our minds and hearts to God, we pray in God's presence. Communion with God originates for Christians in their Baptism into Christ's body, the Church. The Holy Spirit moves us toward union with the Persons of the Trinity and one another. **This communion of life is always possible because, through Baptism, we have already been united with Christ. Prayer is *Christian* insofar as it is communion with Christ and extends throughout the Church, which is his Body. Its dimensions are those of Christ's love (2565).**

Prayer is a marvelous gift from God. It enables us to look at our beloved who is God and it enables us to know that God is constantly looking at us. Through prayer we can empty ourselves and come to know God, not just know about him. Here is a story that can help us understand what prayer is.

A disciple has been calling on God for many years
through prayer, fasting and meditation.
One day she hears a voice within her ask:
"Who is there?"
"At last, at last," she thinks joyfully.
"God," she cries, "It is I. It is I."
But she is met by silence and the voice disappears.
Years pass and the woman goes on meditating
and calling on God with renewed passion.
Suddenly, without warning, she hears the voice again.
"Who is there?"
This time, without hesitation, she replies,
"Only you, only you."
And the door opens and she enters the heart of God.

Source unknown

God is always searching for us, always waiting for us. We may at times feel like we are the ones searching for God or that we have lost contact with God. But God doesn't leave us. We may turn from God at times, but as our loving Father, God tirelessly calls each person to that mysterious encounter known as prayer. **In prayer, the faithful God's initiative of love always comes first; our own first step is always a response (2567).** We need only open ourselves to our Father's love and his tender care.

Sharing Our Faith

- In what ways have I experienced God searching for me?
- How have I experienced prayer as a gift in my life?
- In what ways do I pray? Do I experience a relationship of love in my prayer?
- What will I do to become more faithful to prayer and to my love relationship with the Trinity?

Living the Good News

Determine a specific action (individual or group) that flows from your sharing. This should be your primary consideration.

When choosing an individual action, determine what you will do and share it with the group. When choosing a group action, determine who will take responsibility for different aspects of the action. The following are secondary suggestions:

- Make a commitment to spend at least fifteen minutes a day in prayer if you do not already do so.
- Keep a prayer journal.
- Invite someone to pray with you. For example, if you do not gather as a family for prayer, choose a time to pray together as a family.
- Set up a special room or corner in your home that you designate as a prayer room or prayer corner.
- Research and read good books on prayer and spirituality. Share them with others.

Lifting Our Hearts

Offer spontaneous prayer.

Pray together

Father of kindness and compassion, we have come to the conclusion of this time of prayer and worship. We throw open the windows of our hearts and ask that the peace of your presence may pour out in all directions, touching so many who live without your peace.

Jesus, our Savior, we ask that you extend your peace, binding up the bitterness of painful division, and mending broken hearts and failed friendships. May the realization of your love for us awaken in all people a great desire to serve one another in humble and loving ways. Send your Holy Spirit to call proud hearts to gentleness and inflame hearts that have grown cold. May your blessing extend to all we meet during the days of the coming week. We ask this of you who live and reign as our God, forever and ever. Amen

Adapted from *Prayers for a Planetary Pilgrim*, Edward Hays

Looking Ahead

- Prepare for your next session by prayerfully reading and studying **Session 2, Prayer in the Old Testament** and paragraphs 2566–2597 of the *Catechism*.

Session 2

Prayer in the Old Testament

✝ ✝ ✝

Suggested environment

Bible, candle, and, if possible, the *Catechism of the Catholic Church*
Begin with a quiet, reflective atmosphere.

Lifting Our Hearts

Song
"Here I Am, Lord," Dan Schutte, OCP

Psalm 8
(prayed alternately)

Side 1	O Lord, . . .
	how majestic is your name in all the earth!
Side 2	You have set your glory above the heavens....
	When I look at your heavens, the work of your fingers,
	the moon and the stars that you have established;
Side 1	what are human beings that you are mindful of them,
	mortals that you care for them?
Side 2	Yet you have made them a little lower than God,
	and crowned them with glory and honor....
Side 1	O Lord, . . .
	how majestic is your name in all the earth!

Psalm 8:1, 3, 4, 5, 9

Sharing Our Good News

Share how you did with your Living the Good News from the previous session.

Exploring the *Catechism*

Prayer is a part of our loving relationship with God. Throughout history God has gradually revealed that prayer is **a reciprocal call, a covenant drama. Through words and actions, this drama engages the heart. It unfolds throughout the whole history of salvation (2567). Prayer is bound up with human history, for it is the relationship with God in historical events (2568).** In the Old Testament, we hear about God's loving relationship with us in the events of the lives of various men and women.

In the initial chapters of Genesis, the first book of the Old Testament, we are told that those who were faithful, like Abel, Noah, and Abraham lived in intimacy with God. God was present to them and they were aware of God's presence. Their offerings were **pleasing to God** because their hearts were **upright and undivided.** They placed God first in their lives **(2569).**

God, who has a loving **covenant with every living creature, has always called people to prayer.** There is perhaps no greater revelation of prayer in the Old Testament than that which is revealed to Abraham **(2569).** When God calls Abraham, he goes forth, with an open heart, entirely willing to follow the call of God no matter where it will take him. Abraham responds with an attentive heart. **Abraham's prayer is expressed first by deeds,** and only later does it come in the form of words. God called Abraham and calls us to act according to his will, not merely to say words of commitment. We learn about prayer from this Old Testament story **(2570).**

Scripture: Pondering the Word Genesis 12:1–9 and Genesis 15:1–6

Sharing Question

- Abraham's heart was attuned to God. He not only believed in God, but walked in God's presence. How do you consciously walk in God's presence?

Continued Exploring the *Catechism*

Abraham was a person of great faith. Through him God renews the promise of creation—I am with you always. In a similar manner, God renews the promise made to Jacob who wrestled all night with a mysterious figure before confronting his brother Esau. From the stories of Abraham and Jacob we learn that **prayer** [is] **a battle of faith and...the triumph of perseverance (cf. Genesis 32:24–30; Luke 18:1–8) (2573).** How alive those stories are for us today! So often we struggle to follow God's will in our lives. Sometimes we "wrestle" to understand how to handle certain situations or relationships in our lives. Our spiritual tradition tells us to continue to struggle and persevere in that struggle, recognizing that God is there to help us and to guide us if we only ask.

Continuing our Old Testament reflection on prayer, we encounter Moses whose prayer **becomes the most striking example of intercessory prayer (2574). Here again the initiative is God's. From the midst of the burning bush he calls Moses (Exodus 3:1–10). This event will remain one of the primordial images of prayer in the spiritual tradition of Jews and Christians alike.** Moses is called to be God's messenger, to assist in the work of salvation. But like us, Moses isn't so sure about God's plan. "I can't do it," he says. He makes excuses and questions his call. Yet God says to Moses, "You are the one" and reveals the mighty works Moses will do with God's help **(2575).**

Moses, a humble man, says "yes," and God speaks to him face-to-face, as a person speaks to a friend. Moses' prayer is a contemplative prayer. He knows God intimately. He **converses with God often and at length**, and shares what God has told him with all the Israelites **(2576).** From his **intimacy with the faithful God... Moses drew strength and determination for his intercession** to God to save the people. Moses, through his relationship with God, was able to assure the people who were struggling that indeed God would save them **(2577).**

Intercessory prayer inspires all of us. Intercessory prayer can be mysterious. **God is love** and does not forget. God has given us such great examples through Moses and all the intercessory prayers in our spiritual tradition, that we cannot dismiss the importance of intercessory prayer **(2577).** In fact, the intercessions of Moses foreshadow the prayer of intercession of Jesus **(2593).** The mystery of intercessory prayer is that God wants and does so much more for us than we could ever ask or do for ourselves.

9

The prayer of the People of God flourishes in…God's dwelling place, first the ark of the covenant and later the Temple (2578). The people who came together to pray were guided in their prayer by their leaders—the shepherds and the prophets—especially leaders like King David. **David is…the king "after God's own heart," the shepherd who prays for his people and prays in their name.** In his prayer, David faithfully adheres to God's promise and expresses a longing and joyful trust in God **(2579).**

Hannah begged God for a child and later, offered prayers of gratitude for her son, Samuel: "My heart exults in the LORD, my horn is exalted in my God" (1 Samuel 2:1–10). Judith led Israel in a wonderful song of thanksgiving and praise: "A new hymn I will sing to my God. O LORD, great are you and glorious, wonderful in power and unsurpassable" (Judith 16:1–17).

For the People of God, the Temple was to be the place of their education in prayer…. But ritualism often encouraged an excessively external worship. The people needed education in faith and conversion of heart; this was the mission of the prophets… (2581).

Elijah is the "father" of the prophets… (2582). Like all the prophets, Elijah drew strength from his encounters with God for his mission. The prophets prayed, not to escape from this world, but rather to be attentive to the Word of God and to act on that Word. **At times their prayer is an argument or a complaint, but it is always an intercession that awaits and prepares for the intervention of the Savior God… (2584).**

The Psalms, which are the **masterwork of prayer in the Old Testament,** have both a personal and communal dimension. They **were gradually collected into the five books of the Psalter (or "Praises")… (2585).** The Psalms express and acclaim God's saving works and are a *mirror of* **God's marvelous deeds** in history that are a reflection on **the human experiences of the Psalmist (2587–2588).** We see certain characteristics in the Psalms: **simplicity and spontaneity of prayer; the desire for God…; the distraught situation of the believer who…is exposed to a host of enemies and temptations, but who waits upon what the faithful God will do… (2589).** The Psalms are full of songs of praise and thanksgiving and Psalms can be prayed by people of all times and ages.

We can learn a great deal about prayer from reading and reflecting upon the lives and prayers of our Hebrew ancestors in faith. Their stories are so much like our own. We, too, are called by God to an intimacy based on

10

love and fidelity. We struggle as did the peoples in the Old Testament to know God, not merely to know *about* God. We join the Psalmist often in lamenting our sorrows and praising God, sometimes feeling God's love and other times feeling abandoned, sometimes feeling comfort and other times feeling confusion and fear. Through it all, we recognize we are one family with a history of a powerful relationship with God who always reaches out for us and draws us into a deeper love.

Sharing Our Faith

- Think of a favorite person in the Old Testament. What does his or her life and prayer teach me about prayer?
- What is one situation in my life in which I felt called to persevere in prayer?
- What are some of the intercessory prayers I offer?
- Do I pray the Psalms regularly? If so, what have they meant in my life? If not, what do I feel the merits would be if I prayed them?

Living the Good News

Determine a specific action (individual or group) that flows from your sharing. This should be your primary consideration.

When choosing an individual action, determine what you will do and share it with the group. When choosing a group action, determine who will take responsibility for different aspects of the action. The following are secondary suggestions:

- Read one Psalm daily, reflecting on the words of praise, thanksgiving, supplication, or trust.
- Pray Psalm 131 daily.
- Select one book of the Old Testament to read this week, for example, Ecclesiastes, Amos, Micah.
- Speak with a person from another faith tradition, for example, Jewish, Muslim, Buddhist, to learn more about his or her prayer traditions.

Lifting Our Hearts

Pray spontaneously prayers of gratitude.

Pray Psalm 46 alternately.

Side 1	God is our refuge and strength, a very present help in trouble.

Side 2	Therefore we will not fear, though
	    the earth should change,
	though the mountains shake in
	    the heart of the sea;

Side 1	though its waters roar and foam,
	    though the mountains tremble
	    with its tumult.

Side 2	There is a river whose streams
	    make glad the city of God,
	the holy habitation of the Most
	    High.

Side 1	God is in the midst of the city; it
	    shall not be moved;
	God will help it when the
	    morning dawns.

Side 2	The nations are in an uproar, the
	    kingdoms totter;
	he utters his voice, the earth
	    melts.

Side 1	The LORD of hosts is with us; the God of Jacob is our refuge.

Psalm 46:1–8

Looking Ahead

- Prepare for your next session by prayerfully reading and studying **Session 3, Jesus and Mary Teach Us to Pray** and paragraphs 2598–2622 of the *Catechism*.

Session 3
Jesus and Mary Teach Us to Pray

† † †

Suggested environment
Bible, candle, and, if possible, the *Catechism of the Catholic Church*
Begin with a quiet, reflective atmosphere.

Lifting Our Hearts

Song
"Mary, Full of Grace," Jeanne Frolick, S.F.C.C., OCP

Pray together

> Jesus, teach me how to pray.
> > Let me feel the need for prayer,
> > and an ardent desire to encounter you in life.
> Remake me, open me, strengthen me
> > and increase within me faith, hope, and love.
> Mary, my mother, given to me by your Son,
> > Teach me to pray as you taught him.
> Pray for me, too, O Mary, my mother,
> > That I will be faithful like Jesus.

Sharing Our Good News

Share how you did with your Living the Good News from the previous session.

Exploring the *Catechism*

We can learn the fullness of prayer by contemplating the life of Jesus and listening to what he taught us about prayer **(2598). Jesus learned to pray according to his human heart.** He learned to pray from Joseph, his foster father, and from Mary, **his mother, who kept in her heart and meditated upon all the "great things" done by the Almighty**. Jesus learned to pray in the Jewish traditions of his time—in the synagogue and with the Temple leaders. But the intense prayer of Jesus **springs from an otherwise secret source**, a totally loving God. Jesus knew that already at age twelve when he told his mother and father, "I must be in my Father's house" (Luke 2:49). As God's Son, Jesus teaches us filial prayer, that is, prayer of children toward a loving Father (**2599**).

Jesus prays *before* the decisive moments of his mission: before his Father's witness to him during his baptism and Transfiguration, and before his passion and death. At each juncture in Jesus' life, he went to God the Father and humbly and trustingly committed his human will to God's will (**2600**). Listen to Mark's account of Jesus' prayer after casting out demons.

Scripture: Pondering the Word   Mark 1:32–35

Sharing Question

- In what instances in my life have I gone away to a "lonely place" to pray?

Continued Exploring the *Catechism*

Throughout his life, **Jesus often draws apart to pray *in solitude*, on a mountain, preferably at night (2602).** We are all included in Jesus' prayer. When we read the Scriptures, we learn that **[t]he whole prayer of Jesus is contained in this loving adherence of his human heart to the mystery of the will of the Father (2603).** Jesus begins his prayer with thanksgiving to God, implying that he believes God will always hear his petitions. If we pray as Jesus did, this is how we are to ask: *before* **the gift is given**, we commit ourselves to the One who gives the gift. **The Giver is more precious than the gift… (2604).**

Jesus gave himself totally to his Father. When the time came for his passion and death, Jesus offered his priestly prayer (read John 17). Even though he was afraid for himself, he prayed for the world and those who would follow him. While fearful, he was still willing to freely follow God's will. After great suffering and pain, Jesus prays his final prayer, "Father, into your hands I commit my spirit" (Luke 23:46) (**2604–2605**).

What are we to learn about prayer from Jesus? **Like a wise teacher he takes hold of us where we are and leads us progressively toward the Father.** With his followers, Jesus begins by building on what they know from the Old Covenant. Then he reveals the reign of God in parables, in stories they can understand. Finally he speaks openly of the power of the Spirit who will enable them to pray (**2607**). At the heart of Jesus' message is always conversion of heart. Conversion requires **reconciliation…, love** of enemies, and prayer for persecutors, prayer to the Father in secret, not heaping up empty phrases, prayerful forgiveness from the depths of the heart, purity of heart, and seeking the Kingdom before all else (2608). Once committed to conversion, the heart learns to pray in *faith* (2609).

Jesus calls us not only to conversion and faith, but also to watchfulness in prayer. In prayer, we as disciples keep watch, always attentive to God and the ways God is present in our lives and in our world (2612). From Jesus we learn that one of the great gifts given to us is that we can now ask in Jesus' name. We can know about God through Jesus and through Jesus we are promised that **our petitions will be heard (2614).**

We can learn a lot about prayer from Mary also. The gospel tells **us how Mary prays and intercedes in faith.** It is as she is standing **at the foot of the cross (cf. John 19:25–27),** giving her Son freely, **that Mary is heard as the Woman, the new Eve, the true "Mother of all the living" (2618).** Through her Fiat and Magnificat we learn to give ourselves with our whole being in faith. The Magnificat is the song both of Mary and the entire Church; it is **the song of thanksgiving for the fullness of graces poured out…and the song of the "poor" whose hope is met by the fulfillment of the promises made to our ancestors, "to Abraham and to his posterity for ever" (2619).**

Whenever we are tempted to say we don't know how to pray, we need only look to Jesus and Mary who are our best teachers. Both Jesus and Mary gave themselves totally to God. Their prayers were humble and full of gratitude. In the words of St. Paul, they "prayed constantly" (1 Thessalonians 5:17). Obviously living in the presence of God in a prayerful attitude, they rejoiced in living out the will of God daily. They were "in the marketplace." Jesus and Mary were totally preoccupied with God and were intent on following God's will no matter what the price.

Sharing Our Faith

- What have I learned from the lives of Jesus and Mary that has taught me how to pray?
- What gospel passage tells me how to pray. How has it helped me or how can it help me with my prayer?
- What would I need to do in order to be able to "pray constantly"?

15

Living the Good News

Determine a specific action (individual or group) that flows from your sharing. This should be your primary consideration.

When choosing an individual action, determine what you will do and share it with the group. When choosing a group action, determine who will take responsibility for different aspects of the action. The following are secondary suggestions:

- Make a commitment to read one of the gospels during this coming week.
- Set aside some time each day for quiet prayer.
- Make a commitment to a retreat experience.
- Pray the Magnificat each day for all Church and civic leaders that justice be integral to all their decisions.
- Pray the rosary for those suffering chronic illnesses that cures may be found and that mercy and love will be extended to them.

Lifting Our Hearts

Pray for a few minutes in silence.

Pray together

> Christ be with me, Christ within me,
> Christ behind me, Christ before me,
> Christ beside me, Christ to win me,
> Christ to comfort me and restore me
> Christ beneath me, Christ above me,
> Christ in quiet, Christ in danger
> Christ in heart of all that love me,
> Christ in mouth of friend and stranger.
>
> *Treasury of Prayers*, St. Patrick

Looking Ahead

- Prepare for your next session by prayerfully reading and studying **Session 4, Forms of Prayer** and paragraphs 2623–2649 of the *Catechism*.

Session 4
Forms of Prayer

Suggested environment

Bible, candle, and, if possible, the *Catechism of the Catholic Church*
Begin with a quiet, reflective atmosphere.

Lifting Our Hearts

Song
"Your Faithful Love," *RENEW the Face of the Earth*, Seasons 1 and 2,
OCP

Sharing Our Good News

Share how you did with your Living the Good News from the previous session.

Exploring the *Catechism*

From the day of Pentecost, we, as Church, have been inspired and formed in prayer through the power of the Holy Spirit. Like the early disciples who gathered in the Upper Room, we are called to devote ourselves to prayer **(2623).** We read in the Acts of the Apostles that the first community of believers "devoted themselves to the apostles' teaching and fellowship, to the breaking of bread, and the prayers" (Acts 2:42) **(2624).** But how are we to pray as followers of Christ and members of his Church? What prayer forms are we to use? We need only look at the marvelous liturgical and spiritual traditions in our history to learn various forms of prayer **(2625).**

The *Catechism* focuses on five forms or expressions of prayer for which the Church provides guidance: blessing and adoration, petition, intercession, thanksgiving, and praise. Listen reflectively and carefully to Paul's prayer of blessing.

Scripture: Pondering the Word   Ephesians 1:3–6

Offer spontaneous prayers of blessing and adoration to God for all the goodness you have received. Begin each prayer with, "We bless you, God, for..." or "We adore you, God..."

Sharing Question

- How do I feel when offering prayers of blessing and adoration to God?

Continued Exploring the *Catechism*

Prayers of Blessing and Adoration

Prayers of both blessing and adoration are based on a loving relationship. When we bless God, we acknowledge a magnificent encounter between God and ourselves as human beings. United in dialogue with God, we offer a response to God's gifts; we **bless the One who is the source of every blessing (2626).** Blessing God is a twofold movement: with the help of the Holy Spirit, **we bless him for having blessed us**, and in turn God blesses us **(2627).** When we adore God, we acknowledge the greatness of the God who made us and of Jesus who saved us. We say by our words and attitude, "You, O God, are worthy of our respect and adoration" **(2628).**

Prayer of Petition

Perhaps the prayer with which we are most familiar is the prayer of petition. We so often say to God, "This is what I need." The New Testament offers us many directives on prayers of petition: **ask, beseech, plead, invoke, entreat, cry out, even "struggle in prayer"** (cf. Romans 15:30). In our prayers **of petition we express awareness of our relationship with God.** We need God because we often turn away from God; our petition is a means of turning back **(2629).**

Sometimes we ask God for things or outcomes that we do not receive and we wonder, "Why aren't you listening?" God is listening, but perhaps we may be asking for things that we *want* rather than what we *need*. We may be asking to do our own will, not God's, and hoping God agrees. When we petition God, our first request needs to be asking forgiveness. Asking forgiveness, with all humility, **is a prerequisite for...pure prayer (2631). Christian petition is centered on the desire and *search for the Kingdom*** *to come.* Thus **we pray first for the Kingdom, then for what is necessary to welcome it and cooperate with its coming (2632).** In other words, we pray to do God's will so that awareness of his reign may come more fully into our world. **[W]e share in God's saving love** and come to **understand that** *every need* **can become the object of petition (2633).**

An anonymous author shared the following reflections on prayers of petition:

> I asked God for strength, that I might achieve…
> I was made weak, that I might learn humbly to obey.
> I asked for health, that I might do greater things…
> I was given infirmity, that I might do better things.
> I asked for riches, that I might be happy…
> I was given poverty, that I might be wise.
> I asked for power, that I might have the praise of others…
> I was given weakness, that I might feel the need of God.
> I asked for all things, that I might enjoy life…
> I was given life, that I might enjoy all things.
> I got nothing that I asked for, but everything I had hoped for.
> Almost despite myself, my unspoken prayers were answered.
> I am among all people, most richly blessed!
>
> Adapted

Prayer of Intercession

Intercession is a prayer of petition which leads us to pray as Jesus did (cf. Romans 8:34; 1 John 2:1; 1 Timothy 2:5–8) (2634). In intercessory prayer, we ask on behalf of another. **The first Christian communities lived this form of fellowship intensely (cf. Acts 12:5; 20:36; 21:5; 2 Corinthians 9:14) (2636).** Like that early Christian community, we, as Christians, recognize our call to pray for one another. We pray for all people, for our entire world. We pray for those we love and those we find difficult to love. We pray for those who care for us and those who do us harm. Like all prayer, intercessory prayer is based on love.

Offer prayers of petition and intercession, remembering those with whom you struggle.

Prayer of Thanksgiving

We are called to relate to our God with grateful hearts. St. Paul reminds us in his First Letter to the Thessalonians: "Continue steadfastly in prayer, being watchful in it with thanksgiving" (1 Thessalonians 5:18) **(2638).** Sometimes we may focus too much on asking God, and we forget to be thankful. We must remember that **[t]hanksgiving characterizes the prayer of the Church... (2637).** The word *Eucharist* itself means thanksgiving. **[E]very event and need can become an offering of thanksgiving (2638).**

Take a few moments to reflect on something for which you are grateful. As a group, offer prayers of thanksgiving.

Prayer of Praise

Praise is the form of prayer which recognizes most immediately that God is God (2639). It gives God glory not because of what he has done, but just because God is **(2649).** When we praise God, we join with his Spirit to bear witness to the fact that we are God's children. The Scriptures express awe and delight at the wonders God has done. Praise is the prayer form that embraces all the others and focuses them on the source and goal of all prayer: God **(2639).** United with all the saints and angels, as members of the Church on earth, we sing together songs of praise with faith in a God who loves us beyond all imagining **(2642).**

Sharing Our Faith

- What prayer form do I prefer? How might I become more comfortable with all prayer forms?
- What local or global news event took place this week for which I could pray? What commitment will I make to pray for that event in the coming week?

Living the Good News

Determine a specific action (individual or group) that flows from your sharing. This should be your primary consideration.

When choosing an individual action, determine what you will do and share it with the group. When choosing a group action, determine who will take responsibility for different aspects of the action. The following are secondary suggestions:

- Keep a prayer journal and write various forms of prayer to God.
- Take a walk in nature and offer prayers of praise to God for the beauty of creation.
- Listen to music that praises God.

Lifting Our Hearts

Pray Psalm 103.

Add any prayers of praise you wish.

Looking Ahead

- Prepare for your next session by prayerfully reading and studying **Session 5, The Sources and Way of Prayer** and paragraphs 2650–2682 of the *Catechism*.

Session 5

The Sources and Way of Prayer

✝ ✝ ✝

Suggested environment
Bible, candle, and, if possible, the *Catechism of the Catholic Church*
Begin with a quiet, reflective atmosphere.

Lifting Our Hearts

Song
"Holy Mystery," *RENEW the Face of the Earth*, Seasons 3 and 4, OCP

Pray together this prayer of the Curé of Ars:

I love you, O my God,
and my only desire is
to love you until the last breath of my life.
I love you, O my infinitely lovable God,
and I would rather die loving you,
than live without loving you.
I love you, Lord,
and the only grace I ask is
to love you eternally....
My God, if my tongue cannot say
in every moment that I love you,
I want my heart to repeat it
to you as often as I draw breath **(2658).**

St. John Vianney

Sharing Our Good News

Share how you did with your Living the Good News from the previous session.

Exploring the *Catechism*

Like the Curé of Ars, we are invited to an intimate love relationship with God expressed through prayer. Prayer does not just happen. In order to pray, we must have the will to pray, and we must also learn how to pray. It is the Holy Spirit who teaches us how to pray **(2650)**. We have, in fact, a great legacy of prayer given to us by the Holy Spirit through the Church. We learn to pray through one another. We give one another lessons on prayer through our own contemplation and through sharing the experiences of spiritual realities in our own lives **(2651)**. In addition, we learn to pray by reflecting upon the great gifts God has given to us, especially the gifts of creation and of grace.

We also learn to pray by reading and reflecting on the Word of God, by celebrating the sacramental liturgy of the Church, and through the theological virtues of faith, hope, and charity **(2653–2658)**. The Word of God tells us the story of Jesus and how he prayed **(2653)**. **In the sacramental liturgy of the Church, the mission of Christ and of the Holy Spirit proclaims, makes present, and communicates the mystery of salvation, which is continued in** our hearts when we pray **(2655)**. We enter into prayer by faith. We believe in Christ's return in hope, and we recognize that God's love is the very source of prayer. Listening to one another and the Word of God, participating in the liturgy of the Church, living the theological virtues, and contemplating the gift of creation are prayer sources we can tap at any time.

Prayer internalizes and assimilates the liturgy during and after its celebration (2655).

When do we pray? We are called to pray each day of our lives, to bring each moment and experience of our lives to prayer. God's presence is constantly with us; we can always recognize God in the present moment. It is, in fact, in the present moment that we encounter God **(2659)**.

Scripture: Pondering the Word   Romans 5:1–4

Sharing Question

- How and when have I learned to pray?

Continued Exploring the *Catechism*

One of the great gifts Jesus left us was the ability to pray in his name through the power of the Holy Spirit. **The invocation of the holy name of Jesus is the simplest way of praying always.** When we repeat the name of Jesus often with an attentive heart, we become more aware of loving God, which **transfigures every action in Christ Jesus (2668).**

(As a group, spend ten minutes in quiet reflection. Each person closes his or her eyes and relaxes. The leader asks the members of the group to breathe in the life of the Holy Spirit and breathe out all their cares and worries. Then each person is invited to slowly and silently repeat the name of Jesus over and over for ten minutes.)

Sharing Question

- Share your experience of the quiet Jesus Prayer.

Continued Exploring the *Catechism*

"No one can say 'Jesus is Lord' except by the Holy Spirit" (1 Corinthians 12:3). **Every time we begin to pray to Jesus it is the Holy Spirit who draws us…[to] prayer….Since he teaches us to pray by recalling Christ, how could we not pray to the Spirit too? That is why the Church invites us to call upon the Holy Spirit every day, especially at the beginning and the end of every important action (2670).** We also call on the power of the Holy Spirit to renew us and to help us transform the world and return us to God.

(Take a few minutes as a group to pray together for the power of the Spirit. Pray each line slowly and reflectively, pausing between the two prayers.)

Come, Holy Spirit, fill the hearts of your faithful; and kindle in them the fire of your love.

Alleluia Verse, Pentecost Sunday #4

Heavenly King, Consoler Spirit, Spirit of Truth,
present everywhere and filling all things,
treasure of all good and source of all life,
come dwell in us,
cleanse and save us,
you who are All-Good.

Byzantine Liturgy, Pentecost Vespers, Troparion

Sharing Our Faith

- When do I most often pray to the Holy Spirit?
- How do I call on the Spirit for the needs of the world?

Continued Exploring the *Catechism*

Mary, the Mother of God, has shown us the way to God. In our prayers to Mary, there are generally two movements: **the first "magnifies" the Lord for the "great things" he did for his lowly servant and through her for all human beings (cf. Luke 1:46–55); the second entrusts the supplications and praises of the children of God to the Mother of Jesus… (2675).** Perhaps the best known prayer we have to Mary is the Ave Maria or the Hail Mary, which encompasses these two movements.

Pray the Hail Mary by reflectively reading paragraphs 2676 and 2677 from the Catechism aloud.

Sharing Question

- How might I pray as Mary did?

Living the Good News

Determine a specific action (individual or group) that flows from your sharing. This should be your primary consideration.

When choosing an individual action, determine what you will do and share it with the group. When choosing a group action, determine who will take responsibility for different aspects of the action. The following are secondary suggestions:

- Keep a prayer journal and write a prayer to God each day.
- Pray the Jesus Prayer or pray the rosary daily.
- Commit yourself to praying to the Holy Spirit for the needs of the world. Take the newspaper and ask the Spirit each day to bring God's power into painful situations.
- Work toward having parish ministry groups use faith sharing at their meetings. Encourage them to use *PRAYERTIME: Faith-Sharing Reflections on the Sunday Gospels*, Cycles A, B, or C before every parish meeting. *PRAYERTIME* is available only through RENEW International. Call 888-433-3221 or go to our Web site: www.renewintl.org.

Closing Song

Listen again to the song "Holy Mystery," *RENEW the Face of the Earth*, Seasons 3 and 4, OCP.

Looking Ahead

- Prepare for your next session by prayerfully reading and studying **Session 6, Guides for Prayer** and paragraphs 2683–2698 of the *Catechism*.

Session 6
Guides for Prayer

✝ ✝ ✝

Suggested environment
Bible, candle, and, if possible, the *Catechism of the Catholic Church*
Begin with a quiet, reflective atmosphere.

Lifting Our Hearts

Song
"It First Must Begin with Me," *RENEW the Face of the Earth*, Seasons 1 and 2, OCP

Pray together

> O God, I freely yield all my freedom to you.
> Take my memory, my intellect and my entire will.
> You have given me everything I am or have;
> I give it all back to you to stand under your will alone.
> Your love and your grace are enough for me;
> I shall ask for nothing more.
>
> St. Ignatius Loyola

Sharing Our Good News

Share how you did with your Living the Good News from the previous session.

Exploring the *Catechism*

We can learn a lot about prayer from those who have gone before us. The Letter to the Hebrews refers to people we call saints as **[t]he witnesses who have preceded us into the kingdom** (cf. Hebrews 12:1). These may be people whom the Church has designated as saints or people we have known—friends, family or others who have been witnesses to us. We, as believers, **share in the living tradition of prayer by the example of their lives, the transmission of their writings, and their prayer today.**

They continue to contemplate and praise God, and we believe that they **constantly care for those** of us **whom they have left on earth.** It is only right that we ask them to intercede for us and for our world **(2683).**

Throughout our Church's history various spiritualities have developed— Benedictine, Franciscan, Dominican, Jesuit; ascetical, charismatic, etc. Each developed in a given time and responded to the needs of the time. All of these schools of spirituality provide unique guides for the spiritual life. In their rich traditions, they show different facets of the light of the Holy Spirit. Together they make a beautiful whole **(2684).**

Scripture: Pondering the Word   1 Thessalonians 1:2–10

Sharing Question

- Who are the saints I pray to for intercession? How have they helped me?

Continued Exploring the *Catechism*

There are many places where we receive guidance in prayer. **The *Christian family* is the first place of education in prayer (2685).** Many of us learned our first prayers in our families. Parents are responsible for teaching their children. Praying before meals, praying before going to bed, praying for those who are sick, praying for everyday needs, praying in gratitude and praise for God's wonderful works—these are all ways parents can teach their children to pray. In addition, couples and friends can help one another with prayer by committing themselves to pray together regularly. Prayer can be a great source of strength for any relationship.

Within the Church we also have many guides. We have ordained ministers who are responsible for the formation of others in prayer. They are ordained to lead us in worship, and, through their direction and example, can be wonderful guides for prayer **(2686).** Catechists, too, have a unique opportunity to guide people in prayer. They teach **children, young people, and adults…to meditate on The Word of God in personal prayer,** [practice] **it in liturgical prayer, and** [internalize the gospel message] at all times in their lives **(2688).** In addition, [m]any *religious* **have consecrated their whole lives to prayer**, and provide for the entire Church a source and model of contemplative living **(2687).**

One of the powerful signs of renewal in our Vatican II Church is the emergence of prayer groups that can become "schools of prayer." We see more and more people making the commitment to come together regularly to pray, to reflect together on the Scriptures, and to find ways to live their faith in everyday life **(2689)**.

Another sign of renewal in the Church is the growing interest in spiritual direction and spiritual friendships. In spiritual direction, a person chooses someone to whom the Holy Spirit has given gifts of **wisdom, faith and discernment** to offer assistance and direction in his or her spiritual journey **(2690)**. In spiritual friendship, one person invites another into a mutual relationship, each sharing his or her personal spiritual journey with the other.

We can pray at any place and at any time. However, there are some places that are more conducive to prayer. A church **is the proper place for the liturgical prayer of the parish community. It is also the...place for adoration of...the Blessed Sacrament (2691).** Monasteries, retreat centers, locations of pilgrimage are also places that provide solitude and time **for more intense personal prayer (2691).** Taking time every once in a while to go away to a quiet place can be such an important help on our spiritual journey.

Finally, an important place for prayer is in our own homes. It can be very helpful for families or individuals to set aside a "prayer corner" or some sacred space for prayer. We can create that space in our homes by setting aside a place for a candle, icons, or whatever other symbols lead us to prayer **(2691)**. We are reminded in the Scriptures that Jesus often went away to a lonely place to pray **(2602)**.

Prayer is the life of the new heart. We are to be animated at all times by prayer **(2697)**. We cannot "pray at all times" unless we find specific times to pray. Our spiritual traditions have taught us that daily prayer, **such as morning and evening prayer, grace before and after meals, the Liturgy of the Hours** and most important, Sunday Eucharist, are primary times for prayer **(2698)**. Having a full life of prayer means that we are continually allowing our hearts to be touched by the love and power of God. If we want to grow in our love relationship with God, it is important for us to set aside some time each day to communicate our love and our desire for "new hearts."

Sharing Our Faith

- How did I learn to pray in my family environment?
- What ways do I or could I pray together as a family, as a couple, or with those with whom I live?
- Have I ever gone on a retreat? If so, what was the experience like for me? If not, what would I see as the benefits?
- Do I have a "prayer corner" in my home? If so, how has it helped me in my prayer? If not, where might I make one?

Living the Good News

Determine a specific action (individual or group) that flows from your sharing. This should be your primary consideration.

When choosing an individual action, determine what you will do and share it with the group. When choosing a group action, determine who will take responsibility for different aspects of the action. The following are secondary suggestions:

- Inquire in your parish about future retreats. Register and invite a friend to come along.
- Create a prayer corner in your home.
- Pray for the needs of our world.

Lifting Our Hearts

Offer spontaneous prayers and close with the sign of peace.

Looking Ahead

- Prepare for your next session by prayerfully reading and studying **Session 7, Vocal Prayer and Meditation** and paragraphs 2699–2708 of the *Catechism*.

Session 7

Vocal Prayer and Meditation

Suggested environment
Bible, candle, and, if possible, the *Catechism of the Catholic Church*
Begin with a quiet, reflective atmosphere.

Lifting Our Hearts

Since there will be prayer experiences throughout the session, begin with a few moments of quiet to reflect on God's presence.

Sharing Our Good News

Share how you did with your Living the Good News from the previous session.

Exploring the *Catechism*

As a Church, we have maintained three major expressions of prayer: vocal prayer, meditation, and contemplation **(2699).** In this session we will be focusing on vocal prayer and meditation.

Vocal prayer [praying aloud] **is an essential element of the Christian life.** Jesus taught us the "Our Father," which is vocal prayer, and he prayed aloud often **(2701).** Yet words are not the essence of prayer. St. John Chrysostom, an early Father of the Church, wrote of the importance of our attitude in prayer. He states: "Whether or not our prayer is heard depends not on the number of words, but on the fervor of our souls." Vocal prayer is often the one most accessible when praying in a group. When we share vocal prayer, we help one another both internalize and express the presence of God. Vocal prayer can be **an initial form of contemplative prayer (2704).**

Vocal prayer can be either prayers that we have committed to memory or spontaneous prayers. Take approximately 10 minutes to offer spontaneous vocal prayer aloud to God. Do not rush. Allow intervals of silence between each prayer.

Sharing Question

- How have we, as a group, grown in our comfort with vocal prayer?

Continued Exploring the *Catechism*

It is often said that when we pray, we speak to God; when we meditate, we listen to God. In meditation, we pray in a reflective, imaginative, and relation-centered style. **Meditation is...a quest...to understand the why and how of the Christian life, in order to** respond to God more fully **(2705).** Meditation requires attentiveness. We read something (often the Scriptures), and then we engage our **thought, imagination, emotion, and desire**. We do this **to deepen our convictions of faith, prompt the conversion of our heart, and strengthen our will to follow Christ (2708).** In meditation we listen, trying to be faithful to what God is calling us to do.

Group Meditation

The following suggested format is given for you as a group to use for meditative prayer. Take about twenty minutes. Have one person read the following meditation based on John 4:4–30, the Samaritan Woman. Invite those in the group to use their imaginations to visualize the scene and the people as they enter the story.

My name is Benjamin and I come from Samaria. This is a country just to the north of Israel, and let me tell you, there has been animosity between the Jews and ourselves for a very long time. The Jews do not associate with us, nor we with them. So the story I will tell you today is most unusual, but one very interesting to think about.

I was sitting beside the city well one day around noon, when a very strange thing happened. First a woman came to draw water. Now in our culture, although the well is common to both men and women, they are never to be there together. Women are allowed to come in the morning or evening, but never during the day. That is the time the men are present. But, here at high noon, she arrives. Of course, she had a bad reputation in town because she never observed any decencies that the rest of us adhered to. She probably came at that hour because the other women shunned her.

At any rate, as she was drawing her water, Jesus, who had acquired a reputation as a great preacher, arrived with his followers, at least twelve men. Those men left shortly after they got there. I suppose they went to get some food. That was when a very strange thing happened. Jesus spoke to her; he asked her for some water. Even she admitted this was irregular. "How is it that you, a Jew, ask a drink of me, a woman of Samaria?" For a man to speak to an unaccompanied woman in a public place was very suspicious.

Jesus responded to her: "If you knew the gift of God, and who it is that is saying to you, 'Give me a drink,' you would have asked him, and he would have given you living water."

I perked up my ears at that. "What is he talking about, living water? Maye I could get some too."

Sir," she replied, "You have no bucket and the well is deep. Where do you get that living water? Are you greater than our ancestor Jacob, who gave us the well, and with his sons and his flocks drank from it himself?"

Good question. I wanted to hear the answer to that one.

Jesus replied, "Everyone who drinks of this water will be thirsty again, but those who drink of the ater that I will give them will never be thirsty again. The water that I give will become in them a spring of water gushing up to eternal life."

Jesus' next words surprised me. He told her to go and get her husband. What a sore point this was, since she had had several.

"I have no husband," she replied.

Then Jesus amazed her. "You are right in saying, 'I have no husband, for you have had five husbands, the one you have now is not your husband."

She was stunned and immediately tried to distract him from the truth he had spoken about her personal life by bringing up an ancient religious controversy. She said to him, "Sir, I see that you are a prophet. Our ancestors worshiped on this mountain, but you say that the place where the people just worship is in Jerusalem."

Jesus then proceeded to teach her some very basic truths—it is not important where people worship, but that they worship in spirit and

33

truth. She is an intelligent woman, hungry to learn about God. She listened carefully and drank in everything he said. She had so much to share with him and to ask him. Finally she said, "I know the Messiah is coming. When he comes he will explain everything to us." And Jesus declared, "I am he, the one who is speaking to you."

What a shock for this woman! The apostles returned too and were shocked to see that he was speaking with her. Grace had touched her life. She was a changed woman. She had met Jesus, and believed in him.

She rushed from the well to the marketplace. In her eagerness, she evangelized many in the town who came pouring out to meet this man, Jesus.

This woman was changed in coming to know Jesus and became a disciple.

Sr. Joan Bernier, S.N.D.

Take a few moments of silence as the group reflects on the following questions.

What happened between Jesus and this woman? Why do I think she was so enthusiastic about him? What must it have been like for her to tell the people in the town?

Reflect upon what this says to you in your life.

How have I come to know Jesus? How might my feelings be the same as the woman's? How do I tell my friends about meeting Jesus?

As a group, pray for the power to know God's will and the grace to do his will in your daily life.

Lastly, pray a prayer of thanks to God for his wondrous works.

To summarize the method of meditative prayer: first we read over a passage slowly, staying with the words and images that especially catch our attention; then we imagine the situation and become aware of the feelings and images that are awakened in us; and we end with an expression of our gratitude and love for God.

Sharing Our Faith

- What was this experience of meditation like for me? What touched me the most? What difficulties did I have?
- How might I grow in my commitment to meditation?

Living the Good News

Determine a specific action (individual or group) that flows from your sharing. This should be your primary consideration.

When choosing an individual action, determine what you will do and share it with the group. When choosing a group action, determine who will take responsibility for different aspects of the action. The following are secondary suggestions:

- Set aside twenty minutes every day for meditation on the Scriptures.
- Plan an evening of reflection and meditation with your pastor and/or parish staff and invite the entire parish.
- In your prayer time this week, bring the refugees of the world into God's presence and be in solidarity with them.
- Sponsor a parish seminar on meditation or centering prayer.

Closing Song

"We Walk By Faith," Marty Haugen, GIA

Looking Ahead

- Prepare for your next session by prayerfully reading and studying **Session 8, Contemplative Prayer** and paragraphs 2709–2724 of the *Catechism*.

Session 8
Contemplative Prayer

† † †

Suggested environment
Bible, candle, and, if possible, the *Catechism of the Catholic Church*
Begin with a quiet, reflective atmosphere.

Lifting Our Hearts

Begin with prayers of thanksgiving for God's presence and great gifts. We will not have a formal Lifting Our Hearts in this session since there will be an experience of contemplative prayer later in the session.

Sharing Our Good News

Share how you did with your Living the Good News from the previous session.

Exploring the *Catechism*

What is contemplative prayer? St. Teresa of Avila, the sixteenth-century Spanish mystic and reformer of the Carmelite Order tells us: **"Contemplative prayer [*oración mental*] in my opinion is nothing else than a close sharing between friends; it means taking time frequently to be alone with him who we know loves us"** (St. Teresa of Jesus, *The Book of Her Life*, 8, 5 in *The Collected Works of St. Teresa of Avila*) **(2709).**

In contemplation we are drawn into God's presence; we seek to live in a loving awareness of God. In contemplation we bring our hearts totally into harmony with him. We, in fact, acknowledge that the Holy Spirit is present to pray within us. Contemplation is a great act of love. We desire God as God desires us. We give our hearts unconditionally, and it is within our hearts that we encounter God. We are reminded again that the great mystery is not our love for God, but God's total and unconditional love for us.

In contemplative prayer we seek God whom we love and we seek to serve God in others. We are sought by the God who loves us, not in some impersonal manner, but with true intimacy. In contemplative prayer, the mind and the imagination are less active than in meditation. We are silent and quiet in God's love, an awareness marked by a strong sense of mutual love. In the Song of Songs, one of the wisdom books of the Bible, we have an exquisite poetic expression of the love God has for us. Listen to this beautiful description of God's love for the beloved.

Scripture: Pondering the Word   Song of Songs 2:8–17

Sharing Question

- How do I respond to this love song?

Continued Exploring the *Catechism*

Contemplative prayer is the prayer of the child of God, of the forgiven sinner who agrees to welcome the love of God **(see 2712).** It is a great ***gift,* a grace** [and] **can be accepted only in humility and poverty. Contemplative prayer is a *covenant* relationship established by God within our hearts (2713).**

All we have to do is think about the experience of human love. When we "fall in love" with someone, we are aware of that person's presence. We long to gaze into their eyes. Words are unnecessary. Silence often speaks on a deeper level than words. Contemplative prayer is an intense time of prayer when we gaze on Jesus and come to know in our inner selves an intense love for him **(2714–2715).** In contemplative prayer we don't need words; we simply need to be present to our God.

Contemplative Prayer

Take twenty minutes for contemplative prayer together. Choose an icon or picture of Jesus. Light a candle. Each person is asked in silence to contemplate God's love. When you feel distracted, just bring yourself quietly back to your reflection. During the contemplative prayer, it is suggested that the tape or CD, Laudate, Music of Taizé, *be playing quietly in the background.* Laudate *by Jacques Berthier, Taizé Community, 71520 Taizé, France, can be purchased at most religious bookstores.*

Sharing Our Faith

- What was the experience of contemplative prayer like for me? Share my thoughts and feelings.
- What do I see as the benefits of contemplative prayer?
- How might I make a commitment to contemplative prayer in my everyday life?

Living the Good News

Determine a specific action (individual or group) that flows from your sharing. This should be your primary consideration.

When choosing an individual action, determine what you will do and share it with the group. When choosing a group action, determine who will take responsibility for different aspects of the action. The following are secondary suggestions:

- Commit yourself to contemplative prayer at least once a week.
- Join with others in contemplative prayer.
- Read and study paragraphs 2709–2719 of the *Catechism* on contemplative prayer.

Closing Song

"Ubi Caritas" (or any of the songs on the tape or CD, *Laudate*)

Looking Ahead

- Prepare for your next session by prayerfully reading and studying **Session 9, Difficulties in Prayer** and paragraphs 2725–2758 of the *Catechism*.

Session 9

Difficulties in Prayer

† † †

Suggested environment
Bible, candle, and, if possible, the *Catechism of the Catholic Church*
Begin with a quiet, reflective atmosphere.

Lifting Our Hearts

Song
"Unless A Grain of Wheat," Bernadette Farrell, OCP

Pray alternately

Side 1	By faith, Abraham, when he was tested, believed in the power of God.
Side 2	By faith, Moses left Egypt, and led his people to freedom.
Side 1	By faith, the prophets and other great women and men promoted justice, received promises, shut the mouths of lions, and quenched raging fires (cf. Hebrews 11).
Side 2	By faith early apostles and disciples were tested in every way, yet they believed.
Side 1	By faith, more Christians were martyred in the last century, than in all other centuries combined.
All	Faith is our conviction of things we have not seen (cf. Hebrews 11:1). Without faith, we are afraid, but with faith we can "move mountains." We ask you, God, to increase our faith and make us as strong as those in the early Church. Amen

Sharing Our Good News

Share how you did with your Living the Good News from the previous session.

Exploring the *Catechism*

Prayer is not always easy. While prayer is a gift to us from God, it also requires a response on our part. Sometimes that response is difficult. We all have periods when we don't feel like praying; at times, we probably have tried to pray and felt God's absence, rather than God's presence. The *Catechism* goes so far as to call prayer a "battle." We battle against ourselves and against all that pulls us away from God **(2725).**

What are some of the reasons that prayer is difficult? We may at times have *erroneous notions of prayer*. We may see prayer as **a simple psychological activity**, or a way **to reach a mental void**. We may **reduce prayer to ritual words and postures**. We may even consider prayer to be something incompatible with everything else we have to accomplish. We think we **"don't have the time."** We may even forget **that prayer comes also from the Holy Spirit and not from** ourselves **(2726).**

Prayer is also difficult because many of the attitudes of our society mitigate against it. We **prize production and profit,** so prayer may seem useless. We are bombarded with constant noise, so that reflection and quiet may feel uncomfortable. We may even struggle with the attitude that prayer is an escape from reality or doesn't make sense in a world of reason and science **(2727).** But perhaps our greatest struggle in prayer is that we can easily experience failure in prayer. We can become discouraged **during periods of dryness**. We can be saddened that we have not given ourselves totally to God, disappointed that we have not acted always in accord with God's will. So we can easily ask: **what good does it do to pray? (2728).**

As Christians, we are called to face the struggle. We can face these obstacles to prayer by humility, trust, and perseverance. Listen to these beautiful words of Jesus as told by Matthew.

Scripture: Pondering the Word   Matthew 6:19–34

Sharing Question

- What have been my personal struggles with prayer? How do these words of Jesus help me in that struggle?

Continued Exploring the *Catechism*

We are called to great vigilance in prayer. **When Jesus insists on vigilance, he always relates it to himself, to his coming on the last day**

and every day: *today* **(2730).** No matter what struggle we have, we can always make the conscious choice to be vigilant, to try over and over again. God asks only for our hearts. We do not have to pray perfectly; we need only give our hearts to God with childlike trust.

Two difficulties that those who are vigilant in prayer face at times are distraction and dryness. We can, if we are persevering and trusting, find ways of handling these situations. When we find ourselves distracted, there is no need to analyze the distraction; all we need do is turn our heart back to God. For most of us, distractions are common. The distraction is not as important as our effort to always return to God. We can learn from distractions what we are really attached to and offer that distraction to God, becoming increasingly aware that we want to grow even closer to God. In other words, distractions may serve as part of the offering of ourselves in prayer to God **(2729).**

The same is true for dryness in prayer. We can recognize in those moments of dryness that it is not good feelings alone, but, rather, our faith that brings us to God. Dryness requires faith and continued conversion in our lives **(2731).**

Sometimes we can also face temptations in prayer. Perhaps **[t]he most common…temptation is our** *lack of faith*. We may turn to God at times as a last resort, but do we really believe that we can do nothing without God? **(2732).** How strong is our faith? Another temptation some people face is despair and discouragement. Where is God? **(2733).**

How do we respond when we pray for something and our prayer seemingly goes unheard? When that happens, we might ask ourselves these questions: **"Why do we think our petition has not been heard? How is our prayer heard?" (2734). Are we convinced that "we do not know how to pray as we ought"? (Romans 8:26). Are we asking God for "what is good for us"? (2736).** If we trust God, we will come to understand that our prayers are heard. We may not receive the response we want, but God is loving us and will give us much more than we could ask. Reflect on the words of Evagrius Ponticus and St. Augustine:

"Do not be troubled if you do not immediately receive from God what you ask him; for he desires to do something even greater for you, while you cling to him in prayer" (Evagrius Ponticus). "God wills that our desire should be exercised in prayer, that we may be able to receive what he is prepared to give" (St. Augustine) **(2737).**

Our challenge is to persevere in love and to "pray constantly." St. Paul tells us, "Pray at all times in the Spirit, with all prayer and supplication" (Ephesians 6:18). **This tireless fervor can come only from love (2742).** This love opens us to the following three realities: *It is always possible to pray…. Prayer is a vital necessity….* **Prayer** and *Christian life* **are inseparable (2743–2745).**

No matter where we are, we can pray. We can pray in our cars, as we walk, during conversations with people, while waiting in lines, or at the computer **(2743)**. St. John Chrysostom tells us how vital prayer is to us: "Nothing is equal to prayer; for what is impossible it makes possible, what is difficult, easy" **(2744).** We can unite our work, our lives, our entire beings with God. No matter what our battles or struggles with prayer, as long as we offer our hearts to God, we will be transformed. Slowly, day-by-day, we will come to know more concretely that it is the Spirit who prays in us. We need only be open, trusting, and persevering.

Sharing Our Faith

- How do I handle distractions or dryness in my prayer?
- How have I responded to God when I felt my petitions were not heard? In what ways have I experienced God giving me more than I could ask for or imagine?
- Are there ways I have come to believe that prayer is both possible and necessary?
- How do I experience prayer and the Christian life as inseparable?

Living the Good News

Determine a specific action (individual or group) that flows from your sharing. This should be your primary consideration.

When choosing an individual action, determine what you will do and share it with the group. When choosing a group action, determine who will take responsibility for different aspects of the action. The following are secondary suggestions:

- When distractions arise as you pray, make a conscious effort to turn your heart back to God.
- Pray for the needs of others.
- Keep a prayer journal, acknowledging your struggles in prayer.

Lifting Our Hearts

Offer spontaneous prayers.

Pray together

O Lord, Jesus Christ,
you who said, "I tell you solemnly,
if anyone says to this mountain,
'Get up and throw yourself into the sea,'
with no hesitation in his or her heart,
believing that it will happen, it will be done,"
increase our faith this day.
Let it grow at least to the size of a mustard seed.
Help us, O Lord,
to believe impossible things
and to trust you with our hearts
and not just our heads.
We ask this of you
who live and reign with God our Father
and the Holy Spirit forever and ever. Amen

> Adapted from *Let's Pray*, Charles Reutemann, F.S.C.

Looking Ahead

- Prepare for your next session by prayerfully reading and studying **Session 10, The Lord's Prayer** and paragraphs 2759–2785 of the *Catechism*.

43

Session 10
The Lord's Prayer

✝ ✝ ✝

Suggested environment

Bible, candle, and, if possible, the *Catechism of the Catholic Church*
Begin with a quiet, reflective atmosphere.

Lifting Our Hearts

Song
"Jesus, Come To Us," David Haas, OCP

The leader will invite participants to offer spontaneous prayers of love to God.

Sharing Our Good News

Share how you did with your Living the Good News from the previous session.

Exploring the *Catechism*

Jesus "was praying at a certain place, and when he ceased, one of his disciples said to him, 'Lord, teach us to pray, as John taught his disciples'" (Luke 11:1). It was at this moment that Jesus gave us the prayer that we know so well today as the Our Father. The Our Father, which is also called the Lord's Prayer, is "the summary of the whole gospel" in the words of Tertullian. **It is at the center of the Scriptures (2774).** Therefore, we will spend the final three sessions of this booklet reflecting on this beautiful prayer that Jesus taught us to pray.

We call this prayer **"the Lord's Prayer" because it comes to us from the Lord Jesus, the master and model of our prayer (2775).** St. Augustine expressed the comprehensiveness of the Lord's Prayer: "Run through all the words of the holy prayers [in Scripture], and I do not think that you will find anything in them that is not contained and included in the Lord's Prayer" **(2762).** What a powerful prayer it is! It provides us with not only the words to pray but also a model for prayer. Listen to this very familiar prayer with new ears and hearts open to having the words enter your being more fully than ever before.

Scripture: Pondering the Word   Matthew 6:9–13

Read each verse and then pause for a few minutes, allowing the members of the group to reflect.

Sharing Our Faith

- What statement of Jesus particularly touched me as I listened to the Lord's Prayer read from Scripture? Why?

Continued Exploring the *Catechism*

According to Matthew (chapters 5–7), Jesus presents this prayer to us in his Sermon on the Mount where he sets a context for his life and his mission. He begins his sermon with the Beatitudes, teaching us how to live. He continues by reflecting on Moses and the law. Jesus requires even more of his disciples than the Old Law required. We are to be the "salt of the earth" and "the light of the world." We are to love our enemies and "turn the other cheek." It is in the midst of this **teaching for life** that Jesus teaches us this prayer **(2764).**

In his *Summa Theologiae,* Thomas Aquinas calls the Lord's Prayer "the most perfect of prayers.... In it we ask, not only for all the things we can rightly desire, but also in the sequence that they should be desired. This prayer not only teaches us to ask for things, but also in what order we should desire them" **(2763).**

It can be easy for us as human beings to get into habits. We may be so familiar with the Lord's Prayer that, at times, we do not even pay attention to the words. **But Jesus does not give us a formula to repeat mechanically (cf. Matthew 6:7; 1 Kings 18:26–29) (2766).** Jesus knows the words of God and he also knows our human hearts. He **not only gives us the words** to pray but **at the same time he gives us the Spirit....** It is, in fact, this very Spirit who prays in and through us **(2766).** Each time we pray the Lord's Prayer we are saying, "Yes, Father, through the power of the Holy Spirit, I believe and commit myself to your will."

The Lord's Prayer has always been at the center of the Church's prayer. **The first communities prayed the Lord's Prayer three times a day (2767). [T]he Lord's Prayer is...rooted in liturgical prayer.... [it] is an integral part of the major hours of the Divine Office** and is a key component of the sacraments of Baptism, Confirmation, and Eucharist. Every time we pray the Lord's Prayer, we express not only our own needs, but how we eagerly await the Lord's return **(2768–2772).**

The familiar phrase we hear in our eucharistic liturgies before we pray the Lord's Prayer is "…we have the courage to say." This phrase implies some boldness on our part. It reminds us that only through Jesus and the power of the Holy Spirit can we call God "Father." Because of Jesus, we can always begin our prayer by addressing God as a Father, as one who wishes us to recognize that we are children of a loving God. **In no way is God in man's image. He is neither man nor woman. God is pure spirit in which there is no place for the difference between the sexes. But the respective "perfections" of man and woman reflect something of the infinite perfection of God: those of a mother and those of a father and husband (370).** Because Jesus has *revealed* God to us, we are welcomed into *communion* with God **(2780–2781).** We learn from Jesus that God is someone we can address as "Abba," or "Father."

Through Jesus, we learn not only that God is a loving Father, but also we learn who we are. We have been chosen freely as children of God. In this relationship we are called to **continual conversion and *new life.*** We are called to grow more deeply in God's likeness and grace. We are also called to develop ***humble and trusting heart[s].*** St. Augustine summarizes this love relationship: "What would [God] not give to his children who ask, since he has already granted them the gift of being his children?" **(2784–2785).**

Sharing Our Faith

- When did I first learn the Lord's Prayer? What does the prayer mean to me?
- Who are some people I know who are loving parents? What kinds of characteristics do they have?
- How do I see the Lord's Prayer as a model for living? What change in my life would I like to make to respond to the challenges Jesus offers?

Living the Good News

Determine a specific action (individual or group) that flows from your sharing. This should be your primary consideration.

When choosing an individual action, determine what you will do and share it with the group. When choosing a group action, determine who will take responsibility for different aspects of the action. The following are secondary suggestions:

- If you are a parent, choose an action to show greater love to your child. If your parents are alive, choose an action to show them your love.
- Pray for someone who has offended you. Forgive that person.
- Reach out to children who are in need of love.
- Pray the Lord's Prayer three times a day.

Lifting Our Hearts

Take about ten minutes for a quiet meditation. Pay attention to your breathing. Reflect on the ways God has been a loving Father to you in your life.

Close with vocal prayers of gratitude.

Offer a sign of peace to one another.

Looking Ahead

- Prepare for your next session by prayerfully reading and studying **Session 11, The Lord's Prayer (continued)** and paragraphs 2786–2827 of the *Catechism*.

Session 11

The Lord's Prayer (continued)

✝ ✝ ✝

Suggested environment

Bible, candle, and, if possible, the *Catechism of the Catholic Church*
Begin with a quiet, reflective atmosphere.

Lifting Our Hearts

Song
The Lord's Prayer

Take a few minutes to breathe deeply and relax. Close your eyes. Sing the
Lord's Prayer slowly. Pause between each line.

Sharing Our Good News

Share how you did with your Living the Good News from the previous
session.

Exploring the *Catechism*

"Our Father"

When we pray "Our Father," we express **an entirely new relationship
with God**. We say that we recognize God's wonderful free gift of love to
us and that we believe we truly belong to one another **(2786–2787).** When
we pray "Our Father," we address the entire Trinity because we cannot
pray to God without recognizing God as Father, Son, and Spirit **(2789).**
When we pray "Our Father," we acknowledge that we are a community of
faithful disciples, praying in communion with one another. We are, as was
the early Christian community, "The company of those who believed
[who] were of one heart and soul" (Acts 4:32) **(2790).**

We cannot pray the "Our Father" without recognizing that we who are a
community of disciples live in a society with a strong emphasis on
individualism. We are called to leave that individualism behind and to
exclude no one. If we are sincere when we pray the "Our Father," then we
will let go of all divisions and hatred. We will love all people

unconditionally **(2792).** Listen to the words of Jesus in his Sermon on the Mount.

Scripture: Pondering the Word   Matthew 5:21–26

Sharing Question

- We are instructed by Jesus to be reconciled with those with whom we are at odds. With whom do you need to be reconciled in order to be able to honestly address God as "our" Father?

Continued Exploring the *Catechism*

"Who Art in Heaven"

When we pray to our God who is in heaven, we are not praying to God who is restricted to a certain place or space. We have been told in Scripture that heaven is not only in some distant place but is anticipated here and now. The fullness of eternal life with God begins in our earthly journey. God is with us and within us at all times. We pray to the God in heaven who cannot be settled in a certain space, but transcends every place and everything **(2794). The symbol of the heavens refers us back to the mystery of the covenant we are living when we pray to our Father.** The Scriptures tell us that [i]n Christ...**heaven and earth are reconciled (2795).** We are journeying toward our **true homeland** (heaven) to which we already belong **(2802).**

The Seven Petitions

After we have placed ourselves in the presence of God...and offered prayers of adoration, love, and blessing by saying "Our Father who art in heaven," we offer ourselves to **the Spirit...**[who] **stirs up in our hearts seven petitions,** [or] **seven blessings.** In the first three petitions, "Hallowed be thy name," "Thy kingdom come," "Thy will be done on earth as it is in heaven," we glorify God. In the last four petitions, "Give us this day our daily bread," "And forgive us our trespasses, as we forgive those who trespass against us," "And lead us not into temptation," "But deliver us from evil," we recognize our need for God's grace **(2803).**

By the three first petitions, we are strengthened in faith, filled with hope, and set aflame by charity **(2806).**

"Hallowed Be Thy Name"

When we pray the first petition, we acknowledge God's holiness and how we wish to treat him in a holy manner. When we recognize God's power and the marvelous way he has saved us, we can do nothing else but proclaim the holiness of God **(2807).** We live intimately with God, reverencing his name, living in awe of his goodness. But this petition is not only about recognizing God's holiness. It is also about being aware that he is within each of us, and therefore, God's name is "hallowed in us" **(2814).** As we realize that truth more deeply, we cannot help but live holier lives and reverence one another. Our names are very important to each of us, and when we love and are loved, we speak and hear our own names with great reverence.

"Thy Kingdom Come"

In this second petition we pray for God's reign or kingdom to come. We pray for the final coming, but we also pray for God's reign to come "today." God's reign, which is one of "righteousness and peace and joy in the Holy Spirit," is so desperately needed today (Romans 14:17) **(2819).** We are all called to live lives of righteousness, peace, and joy. Our duty as Christians is **to put into action in this world the energies and means received from the Creator to serve justice and peace (cf. *Gaudium et spes* 22; 32; 39; 45; *Evangelii nuntiandi* 31) (2820).** We pray in great hope for the reign of God to permeate ourselves and our world.

"Thy Will Be Done on Earth as It Is in Heaven"

In the third petition, we ask our Father to unite our will to that of his Son, so as to fulfill his plan of salvation in the life of the world (2860). Jesus has told us clearly what God's will is for each of us. We are to "love one another; even as I have loved you, that you also love one another" (John 13:34) **(2822).** Sometimes it may seem difficult to know exactly what God's will is for us. Even if we do have a sense of God's will, we find it difficult at times to give up our own wills. We may feel like we know what is better for us. Like Jesus, we may ask our Father to take away our suffering or pain. But also, like Jesus, we promise in prayer to follow his will. "Not my will, but yours be done" (Luke 22:42).

Doing God's will is not always easy. We are, in fact, incapable of doing his will without the power of the Holy Spirit. With the Holy Spirit, however, we can surrender our will to God's. Through **prayer we can** discern **"what is the will of God"** and be given the grace to do it **(Romans 12:2; cf. Ephesians 5:17; cf. Hebrews 10:36) (2826).**

Sharing Our Faith

- Because we are a community of disciples who call God "Our Father," how are we to relate to all peoples of various cultures, races, and religions of the world?
- How do I feel when people know and respect my name?
- What can I do to help bring about greater love, justice, and harmony in the world?
- What changes do I want to make in my life to follow better the will of God?

Living the Good News

Determine a specific action (individual or group) that flows from your sharing. This should be your primary consideration.

When choosing an individual action, determine what you will do and share it with the group. When choosing a group action, determine who will take responsibility for different aspects of the action. The following are secondary suggestions:

- Look up the meaning of your name. Thank God for the unique gift of life that is yours.
- Speak with a spiritual friend or guide who can help you reflect on God's will in your life in a particular situation.
- Participate in a local situation such as a political campaign that will help bring about greater peace, justice, and harmony in the world.

Lifting Our Hearts

Offer spontaneous prayers.

Invite one person to pray slowly the Lord's Prayer as recorded in Luke's Gospel 11:2–4.

> Father, hallowed be your name,
>   Your kingdom come.
> Give us each day our daily
>   bread
> And forgive us our sins,

for we ourselves forgive
    everyone in debt to us,
And do not subject us to the time
    of trial.

Looking Ahead

- Prepare for your next session by prayerfully reading and studying **Session 12, The Lord's Prayer (continued)** and paragraphs 2828–2865 of the *Catechism*.

Session 12

The Lord's Prayer (continued)

† † †

Suggested environment
Bible, candle, and, if possible, the *Catechism of the Catholic Church*
Begin with a quiet, reflective atmosphere.

Lifting Our Hearts

Song
"The Cry of the Poor," John Foley, OCP

Pray together

> Father,
> we depend on you for all our needs.
> We pray that you "give us this day our daily bread"
> knowing that we belong to you and you to us.
> We believe that we are asking
> for far more than bread,
> and that all our needs
> of body and spirit
> will be met.
> We are asking for the nourishment
> of all who are hungry.
> We pray that you "forgive us our trespasses,
> as we forgive those who trespass against us,"
> that we be forgiven to the extent that we forgive others!
> We know, Lord, how impossible this is for us to do;
> we know that this will be done because,
> with you, "all things are possible."
> Holy Spirit
> of discernment and strength,
> "lead us not into temptation."
> Help us in our struggle between good and evil
> to choose well and to know
> we can do so only by the power of prayer.
> We pray to be freed from all evils,

present, past and future.
We praise and thank you, Father.
"for the kingdom, the power and the glory are yours,
now and forever. Amen"

Sharing Our Good News

Share how you did with your Living the Good News from the previous session.

Exploring the *Catechism*

The final four petitions of the Lord's Prayer remind us of our great need for our Father's help and grace. God is the Creator; we are the creation. When we pray "Give us," we are proclaiming our childlike trust in God. We look to him **for everything** [that] **is beautiful.** Jesus teaches us to ask because in doing so we acknowledge how good God is **(2828).** When we say "Give us," we are also expressing the covenant relationship we have with our Father. We belong to God and God belongs to us **(2829).**

In the Gospel of Luke, Jesus instructs us on prayers of petition. We are encouraged to be persistent in our asking.

Scripture: Pondering the Word   Luke 11:5–13

Sharing Question

- In what ways am I persistent in prayer?

Continued Exploring the *Catechism*

"Give Us This Day Our Daily Bread"

Asking is not always easy because we often prefer to be self-sufficient. We would rather do things ourselves. Yet throughout all of human history, we have learned that we are dependent upon God for all our needs. We are, in fact, dependent upon him for our very life. We ask for bread because we need nourishment to live. But when we ask for bread, we are really asking for more than just bread; we are asking for all of our living needs. And the Father who created us **give**[s] **us the nourishment life requires—all appropriate goods and blessings, both material and spiritual (2830).**

We ask for nourishment not only for ourselves but also for all who are hungry. This prayer has very deep meaning for a world in which, in spite of the fact that there is enough food produced to feed the entire world, thousands of children die each day of starvation. We are reminded that **[t]he drama of hunger in the world calls Christians who pray sincerely to exercise responsibility toward their brethren,** both in their own actions and in **solidarity with the human family (2831).** "Our daily bread" is not for us individually; it **is the "one" loaf for the "many."** We are called as Christians **to communicate and share both material and spiritual goods, not by coercion but out of love, so that the abundance of some may remedy the needs of others (2833).**

St. Ignatius Loyola reminded us that we are to "[p]ray as if everything depended on God and work as if everything depended on [us]" **(2834).** We cannot just pray for bread and not help provide bread for those who are hungry. Today we face many opportunities to care for others. We all eat from the "one" loaf given to us by our Father.

When we pray, "Give us this day our daily bread," we are praying not only for our physical needs but for our emotional and spiritual needs as well. Mother Teresa said that the greatest poverty in the United States is spiritual poverty. **There is a famine on earth,** "not [only] a famine of bread, nor a thirst for water, but of hearing the words of the LORD" (Amos 8:11) **(2835).** We are deeply in need of spiritual nourishment. Today many are struggling to find meaning in their lives. We petition in the Lord's Prayer for this meaning. We can ask for our needs at any time and God will hear us. We, in fact, ask only for our daily bread—what we need for today **(2837).**

"And Forgive Us Our Trespasses, as We Forgive Those Who Trespass against Us"

We have all been hurt and we have all hurt others. Jesus seemed to understand how difficult it is for us as human beings to truly forgive ourselves and one another. It is easy to see when someone has wronged us; it is more difficult to see when we have wronged someone else. In this petition, we ask for God's forgiveness while reminding ourselves that we will experience God's forgiveness only to the degree that we forgive others **(2838).**

We know that we are still sinners, and, like the Prodigal Son and tax collector, we recognize our need for God's mercy **(2839).** But God's forgiveness **cannot penetrate our hearts as long as we have not forgiven** those who have trespassed against us (2840). Those who have tried to forgive themselves or others know it isn't easy—in fact, for us as human beings, it is impossible. But "with God all things are possible" (Matthew 19:26) (2841). We must forgive over and over again. Forgiveness is also one of our daily needs.

"And Lead Us Not into Temptation"

When we pray "lead us not into temptation" **we are asking God not to allow us to take the path that leads to sin (2863).** The word *lead* in **Greek means both "do not allow us to enter into temptation" and "do not let us yield to temptation."** It is important for us to understand that God does not tempt us. God **wants to set us free from evil (2846).** We ask God, however, to help us in our battle between good and evil, not only as individuals but also as a world community.

This petition implores the Spirit of discernment and strength; it requests the grace of vigilance and...perseverance (2863). At many times in our lives we have to make a decision between good and evil, between right and wrong. Choosing good becomes possible only through prayer. Jesus sent the tempter away in the desert by prayer **(2849).** He was constantly vigilant. It is the power of the Holy Spirit that will keep us vigilant and persevering in our struggle to choose between good and evil.

"But Deliver Us from Evil"

In this final petition of the Lord's Prayer, we are asking for deliverance from **Satan, the Evil One...who opposes God (2851).** Jesus won the victory over evil, yet we, today, are still influenced by hatred, vengeance, and all evil. **[W]e pray...to be freed from all evils, present, past, and future** and join in showing forth the victory of Jesus **(2854).**

"For the Kingdom, the Power and the Glory Are Yours, Now and Forever. Amen"

This final doxology, which some Christians use to close the Our Father, proclaims again our adoration and thanksgiving to God. Finally, we say, "Amen," which means, "So be it," or "Yes, God." By this Hebrew word, we express faith and ratify the meaning of the preceding prayer for our lives. We proclaim each time we pray the Lord's Prayer that we believe in a God who loves us and cares for us. We want to praise and thank him and recognize our total dependence on our loving Father.

Sharing Our Faith

- What nourishment am I asking for when I pray "give us this day our daily bread"?
- What can I do for the hungry of my area or the world?
- Whom do I need to forgive at this moment in my life? How will I offer forgiveness?
- With what kinds of temptations am I struggling? How can I rely more on God to help me with these temptations?

Living the Good News

Determine a specific action (individual or group) that flows from your sharing. This should be your primary consideration.

When choosing an individual action, determine what you will do and share it with the group. When choosing a group action, determine who will take responsibility for different aspects of the action. The following are secondary suggestions:

- Continue to meet as a small community. There are three other booklets in this *Why Catholic? Journey through the Catechism* Series that you may wish to consider. They are *The Profession of Faith, The Celebration of the Christian Mystery*, and *Life in Christ*.
- Become a member of Bread for the World.
  Bread for the World
  50 F Street, NW, Suite 500
  Washington, DC 20001
  Phone   800-82-BREAD (800-822-7323) or 202-639-9400
  Fax   202-639-9401
  Web site   www.bread.org
  E-mail   bread@bread.org.
- Work for legislation for a world food bank.
- Journal about those things for which you need to forgive yourself.
- Receive the sacrament of Penance and reconcile with all those you have offended or who have offended or hurt you.
- Review reflectively the major temptations you have in your life. Pray and fast, asking God to help you overcome those temptations.

- Gather as a group to hold a special prayer and social experience to celebrate your faith, your sharing, and your Living the Good News.
- Celebrate in a special way with your group through a prayer or social event.

Lifting Our Hearts

Offer prayers of thanksgiving and praise to God.

Respond to each prayer: How great and glorious is our God!

Conclude by praying the Our Father slowly.

Looking Ahead

- Over 30 other faith-sharing titles are available through RENEW International
  1232 George St.
  Plainfield, NJ 07062-1717
  Phone   908-769-5400 (information)
                   888-433-3221 (orders only)
  Fax   908-769-5660
  Web sites www.renewintl.org.
                   www.ParishLife.com
  E-mail   Resources@renewintl.org

Music Resources

GIA Publications, Inc.
7404 South Mason Avenue
Chicago, IL 60638
Phone   800-442-1358 or 708-496-3800
Fax   708-496-3828
Web site   www.giamusic.com
E-mail   custserv@giamusic.com

Laudate, Music of Taizé
Jacques Berthier
Taizé Community
71520 Taizé, France
This tape/CD can be purchased at most religious bookstores.

Oregon Catholic Press Publications (OCP)
5536 NE Hassalo
Portland, OR 97213
Phone   800-LITURGY (548-8749)
Fax   800-4-OCP-FAX (462-7329)
Web site   www.ocp.org
E-mail   liturgy@ocp.org